Focus on Body Image

How You Feel About
How You Look

Maurene J. Hinds

Enslow Publishers, Inc.

40 Industrial Road	PO Box 38
Box 398	Aldershot
Berkeley Heights, NJ 07922	Hants GU12 6BP
USA	UK

Library of Congress Cataloging-in-Publication Data

Hinds, Maurene J.
    Focus on body image : how you feel about how you look / Maurene J.
Hinds.
        p. cm. — (Teen issues)
    Summary: Discusses how young people feel about the way they look, the
impact of society and advertisers on an individual's body image,
problems with poor self-esteem, and maintaining a healthy body image.
    Includes bibliographical references and index.
    ISBN 0-7660-1915-2
    1. Body image in adolescence—Juvenile literature. 2. Self-esteem in
adolescence—Juvenile literature. [1. Body image. 2. Self-esteem.] I.
Title. II. Series.
BF724.3.B55 H56 2002
306.4—dc21

                                             2001007714

Printed in the United States of America

10 9 8 7 6 5 4 3 2 1

To Our Readers: We have done our best to make sure all Internet Addresses in this book were active and appropriate when we went to press. However, the author and the publisher have no control over and assume no liability for the material available on those Internet sites or on other Web sites they may link to. Any comments or suggestions can be sent by e-mail to comments@enslow.com or to the address on the back cover.

Every effort has been made to locate all copyright holders of material used in this book. If any errors or omissions have occurred, corrections will be made in future editions of this book.

Illustration Credits: Corbis Corporation, pp. 27, 37, 54; Corel Corporation, p. 34; Diamar, p. 32; Donald A. Williamson, p. 14; Enslow Publishers, Inc, pp. 17, 24; Matthew J. Yovich, pp. 6, 11; Skjold Photos, p. 52; U.S. Department of Agriculture, p. 100.

Cover Photo: Skjold Photos.

Contents

1

What Is Body Image?

"I love the looks I get when I am out in public. People stare, call me a freak, but at least I'm an individual. I look for friends who are real, not those who try to fit into some idea of what someone else says they should be. I don't follow the crowd."

Sean, seventeen, smiles, revealing the fanged teeth he had specially made by a dentist. Hooked onto a retainer, they look incredibly real, and were form fitted from a molding of his real teeth. He is dressed head to toe in black: a long coat, metal-spiked "collar" and bracelets, ripped shirt, black pants, and heavy boots. His ears are pierced. His hair, now short, used to be so long he could sit on it. "I've always been different, an outcast. It used to bother me, but now I don't care. This is who I am. I look this way because it's fun.

"I started wearing the teeth for a vampire role-playing game that I do. Then I decided I liked the looks I got when

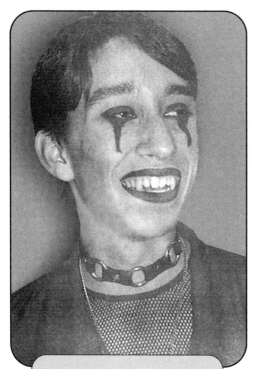

One way for teens to express a positive body image is by having the confidence to dress in any style they are happy with.

wearing them, so now I keep them in most of the time." Sean is also into martial arts. "I like being in shape. I feel better this way. Tae kwon do keeps me strong and flexible." He smiles again. "And the girls like it."[1]

What Is Body Image?

Body image is the way a person feels about his or her body. It is the mental picture a person has about his or her body, influenced by attitudes and feelings about the body.[2] Body image includes feelings about the entire self, from facial features and hair to body size and height. When people say things like, "I'm having a good hair day," they are referring to body image. Many people who participate in sports and physical activity report feeling good about their bodies. A person does not have to have a "perfect" body to feel good about it.

The Body—A Work of Art or a Work in Progress?

Bodies come in many shapes, sizes, and colors. The distinct features of the body and face allow us to tell one person from another. These differences are part of what makes each person unique. People use their bodies for expression: from self-expression in sports or dance to self-expression through hairstyles. However, in today's society, many people try to make their bodies fit an "ideal" look.

Throughout history, the body has been a subject of art and a focus in social, cultural, and religious ceremonies. From famous paintings depicting the body as a work of art to tribal members painting their faces in religious ceremonies, the human form has performed an important cultural and social role.

Over the last hundred years, in western cultures, the image of the ideal body has changed dramatically, especially the way a woman's shape is viewed. In the span of human history, a hundred years is not very long. From prehistoric times, the female body was shown as round and fleshy. Early figurines, depicting goddesses, display the female as a curvy, full-breasted figure.[3] Many artists such as Rembrandt (1606–1669) show fleshy, robust women in their paintings. "Actress Lillian Russell, who was considered the most desirable woman of the 1890s, weighed 200 voluptuous pounds," writes author and researcher Terry Poulton.[4] Marilyn Monroe, one of the most famous movie stars of all time, showed off curves in the 1940s and 1950s that might be viewed as overweight today.

The ideal man's body has remained slightly more constant, but the pressure to be muscular and physically fit may be greater now than ever before. Michelangelo (1475–1564), a famous artist, created the sculpture *David* (1501–1504), showing the male body in great form, complete with a "six pack"—the visible top six sections of the abdominal muscle. However, "David" would have a hard time matching the muscular bodies of current models and athletes.

The pressure to have a "perfect" body can be seen everywhere: advertisements, television shows like *Friends,* and books and magazines filled with advice on losing weight and dieting. Just as girls grow up seeing the unnatural figure of Barbie, boys grow up playing with action figures whose muscles are huge. Some are so muscular that even with drugs and surgery a real man could not attain that size. Many young people are also pressured by friends and family to look a certain way. During adolescence, when the body goes through many changes, the extra burden to be thin and fit can be very hard to deal with.

Self-Expression: A Message to the World

The ways in which people express how they feel about their bodies are as different as each person. Hairstyles, clothing choices, makeup, posture, and jewelry are all ways people use their bodies to express who they are.

Trends come and go, but the body remains the same. Poulton writes, "[Women's bodies] have been pushed, pulled, wrapped, strapped, and caged throughout history."[5] Hairstyles have changed from elaborate wigs to purple Mohawks. Some clothes show off the body, while others hide it. The way someone displays his or her body, from head to toe, says a lot about that person.

Body Talk

Body language, how a person holds his or her body, also says a great deal. According to researchers, people who use a few, selective hand and body gestures when talking appear more powerful. On the other hand, people who feel powerless may draw their bodies in toward themselves by holding their arms in close and keeping their legs tightly together.[6] Body language can be a sign about how people feel about themselves.

Body Image Issues

Body image problems can occur when a person does not like something about his or her body. This can lead to extreme behaviors, which may include excessive dieting to lose weight, taking steroids to increase muscle size, or even resorting to surgery to correct a real or imagined flaw. Behaviors such as these can be related to body image disorders, such as anorexia nervosa (intentionally starving oneself), bulimia nervosa (eating large amounts of food and then vomiting, using laxatives, and/or exercising excessively to get rid of the extra calories). A person's self-esteem can be seriously affected by body image problems. But for every person who has a severe problem with body image, many more suffer to a lesser degree.

What Causes Body Image Problems?

No one knows for sure what causes body image problems, although these issues often start in adolescence. The cause seems to be a combination of psychological, physical, and social factors. The onset of puberty, and all the changes that occur, may be part of the problem. The age at which a person goes through puberty, the time when adolescents reach sexual maturity, can also have an effect on feelings about the body. Studies have shown that girls who go through puberty earlier than their peers have more problems with body acceptance.[7] This may be due in part to the higher rate of teasing that girls may hear from their peers, especially about breast size.[8] On the other hand, boys who go through puberty early have a higher rate of body satisfaction. This may be partly because after puberty, males have more muscle mass.[9]

Pressures from families may also contribute to body image problems. "In families in which there is an eating-disordered child there is a common thread: The existing rules and practices that bind the family together are not [helpful to] the shifting needs of the individual members."[10] For example, rules about expressing or not expressing feelings and rules regarding weight and food can directly influence a person's body image.

Other theories on what causes problems about body image focus on how the brain works. There is some agreement among researchers about the possibility of the brain not functioning correctly, but there is disagreement about exactly what the malfunction is. Chemical imbalances in the brain may also be important, because medications that affect serotonin levels in the brain, which affect feelings of well-being, seem to be helpful.

Still other theories involve the media and gender and effects on self-image. Researchers study topics such as the effects of advertisements on body image, societal beliefs in general, and the way males and females react differently to these things. Some people seem to be more influenced by outside pressures than others.

Research on Gender and Racial Differences of Body Image

Both males and females can have body image problems. Females tend to be more concerned with being thin, while males have more concerns about muscle size. Ironically, many studies have shown that boys' and girls' ideas of what is attractive to the opposite sex are wrong. When shown pictures of male bodies ranging from very thin to large and muscular, boys think that girls find a very large and muscular body to be attractive. In reality, girls pick someone in the middle. Similarly, girls usually pick a very thin woman as what they think the boys will find attractive. The boys actually pick someone with a higher level of body fat.[11]

Some studies have shown differences related to race as well, although those differences may be changing. Some research shows that African-American females are not as concerned with weight and dieting as are Caucasian females.[12] Other studies have shown that Mexican-American females have similar body image problems as Caucasian females, who have the highest level of body dissatisfaction of all the groups tested.[13]

Who Is at Risk for Body Image Problems?

Images of "perfect," thin, and in-shape bodies are everywhere, creating the possibility for almost anyone to develop body image concerns. However, some people are at a higher risk than others.

The need to reach perfection is very strong for some people. While the outcomes can be good, this obsessive behavior can lead to problems. Eating disorders can also result from a need to be perfect.

Athletes in certain sports, such as gymnastics, may feel pressure to maintain a specific body shape and size.

Certain sports place a lot of importance on body shape and size. Athletes in gymnastics, dance, and wrestling are at a high risk for developing disorders. In dance, for example, the ideal body for females is long and lean. The males need to be strong enough to lift ballerinas and do big jumps. They need to perform difficult strength moves in gymnastics. For wrestlers, the desire to weigh in at a set point can lead to extreme dieting and weight-loss methods—or extreme measures to gain weight or develop their muscles.

In a Nutshell

The body can be used as a canvas to express to the world who a person is and how he or she feels about him or herself. In a society that views being thin and in shape as the ideal body, many teens have negative body images, which can lead to other serious problems. In addition, the onset of puberty in adolescence can make it difficult for a teenager to maintain a positive body image.

2

Body Image Disturbances

Researchers do not know exactly what causes body image disorders. Most likely, these disorders stem from a variety of experiences, personal beliefs, and emotional states.

Methods of Testing Body Image

Having a person look at some drawings of various body sizes and then choose one that is believed to be the most accurate drawing of his or her body size is a standard test of body image. Often, people will choose an image of themselves that is too large. Some researchers believe the overestimation of size is a result of an inability to visualize space and size accurately. Others believe that the difference between reality and size estimation is a neurological disorder—when a person sees him or herself as being large, it is actually a delusion, or imagined to be real.[1] Some researchers believe that as a person's body changes, the ability to recognize the changes

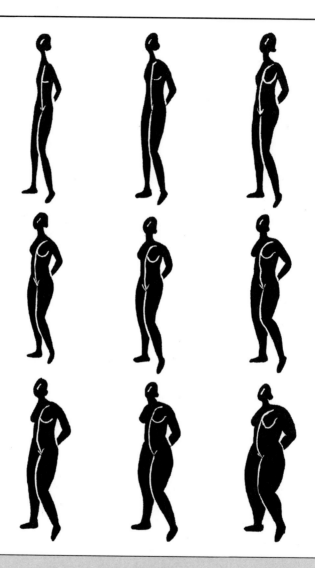

In a study led by Donald Williamson, a group of university students were asked to choose which image looked most like their body. Bulimic students saw themselves as larger than a group of nonbulimic students that was matched for height and weight.

may not happen as fast as the physical changes. Other testing methods measure how satisfied a person is with body size or a specific body part.[2]

Societal Influences

Researchers L. J. Fabian and J. K. Thompson, who study body image issues, found that "teasing was related significantly to body satisfaction, eating disturbance, and self-esteem," and "adolescents with eating disturbances had a greater history of being teased by peers" than others who showed no signs of bingeing or purging.[3] Other factors, such as negative comments from others on food choices, have similar effects.[4]

Cultural Influences

Other theories look to the cultural ideals in our society. Women are expected to look thin, young, and beautiful. Men are expected to be handsome and muscular. Images of these "ideals" can be seen everywhere. Not only is the "perfect" body idealized, but those who do not fit the ideal are often feared and rejected. Making fun of overweight people is often regarded as "okay," even though it is a form of prejudice.

Some studies have shown that when people, especially women, view pictures of thin models, their satisfaction with their own bodies goes down. On the other hand, when shown pictures of larger models, they feel better about themselves.[5] When the differences in the perceived ideal and one's own body are greatly different, increased body dissatisfaction results. These idealized images are culturally accepted as something to strive for, yet few people actually look that way, and even fewer can attain that ideal.

While no one theory can explain why a person has a problem with body image disturbance, the theories can give insight into why some people have more difficulty than others.

Body Dysmorphic Disorder

Body dysmorphic disorder is "a preoccupation with an imagined or slight defect in one's physical appearance,"[6] which often includes the nose, hair, skin, and mouth.[7] Body dysmorphic disorder often starts in adolescence and can be disruptive.[8] A person with body dysmorphic disorder obsesses about something concerning appearance, which he or she thinks is a flaw, and believes that flaw to be more exaggerated than it really is. No one knows exactly what causes this disorder, but some researchers believe that outside factors, such as pressure to look a certain way, can contribute to those feelings of ugliness.

Some of the signs of body dysmorphic disorder are very similar to those shown by people with obsessive-compulsive disorders, such as having obsessive thoughts. The treatments are similar for both conditions, using therapy to try to change behavior. The same medications, antidepressants that help the brain utilize serotonin, are also used to treat both conditions.[9] Some research links body dysmorphic disorder to other serious problems, such as social phobia and major depression.[10]

People will often go to great lengths to correct or rid themselves of the perceived flaw, such as avoiding social situations, pulling out their hair or picking at the "flaw," and seeking surgery (often multiple surgeries). These actions do not solve the problem. Even with surgery, a person with body dysmorphic disorder may believe that the problem still exists or is worsened.[11] The effects of body dysmorphic disorder range from low self-esteem to suicide.[12]

Anorexia Nervosa

Anorexia nervosa more commonly affects girls (between one and 4 percent of young women),[13] but boys are affected as well. Anorexia nervosa is characterized by a refusal to maintain a healthy body weight, a fear of gaining weight, loss of menstruation (amenorrhea) in females, and a distorted sense of how one looks.[14] People suffering from anorexia nervosa have a low body weight, about 15 percent or more below the normal weight for their height.[15] Additionally, those with anorexia nervosa may experience "constipation, abdominal pain, cold intolerance, lethargy, anxious energy, fatigue and headaches."[16] Body hair, called lanugo, may appear on those who have lost a lot of body weight to help keep the body warm because body fat is so low.

People with anorexia nervosa often do not realize they have a problem, and they cannot see that they are very thin. A person with anorexia nervosa believes that his or her body is bigger than it actually is, regardless of weight.

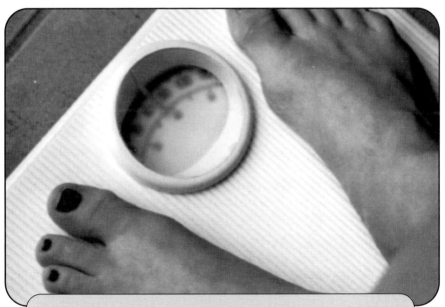

People who suffer from an eating disorder often do not like what they see when they step on the scale. No matter what the scale reads, the person still tends to feel overweight.

Daniel's Story

When Daniel was nine years old, he started becoming worried about the fat content in his diet. "It started out that I would try and only eat foods low in fat. I wanted to be healthier. I would read the labels on everything I ate. Then one day I decided that if low fat was good, no fat was even better." Daniel, now twelve, describes his concerns about fat as something that just "clicked on" inside his head one day. "I started thinking that I was fat. After a while, I would skip lunch at school and barely eat anything for dinner." Over the course of the next few months, he greatly reduced the amount of food he ate and lost a lot of weight, and his parents became very worried.

"I was always tired and weak, like when you have the flu. And I would get depressed and sad, even over little things. And I thought things happening around me were my fault. If a friend of mine got in trouble, I would feel guilty, thinking that I could have done something to prevent it. Part of me knew I needed to eat more, but another part of me kept saying I was fat and bad. That part kept getting louder while the other voice got quieter. When people told me I was skinny, I took it as a compliment."

Daniel also showed typical signs of anorexia. He tried to be perfect in everything he did. He enjoyed watching other people eat, even though he was starving himself. Eventually, Daniel was hospitalized. The hospital staff inserted a tube through his nose and into his stomach for liquid food. Later, he was sent out of state for treatment. Unfortunately, the treatment center did not have any places for boys that young with eating disorders, so he was placed with psychiatric patients, which did not help.

After leaving the treatment facility, Daniel found the people who eventually helped him. He did extensive counseling with two nutritionists and found a doctor who prescribed Luvox, an antidepressant. This combination, along with his love of baseball, helped Daniel find the way out of his disorder. He knew that, in order to play baseball, he needed physical strength. Over time, with the help of nutritional counseling and medication, he overcame his fear of food. He now enjoys playing baseball and eating a wide variety of foods. Daniel's story has a happy ending.

"I now know that what counts is who you are on the inside. It doesn't matter whether you are heavy, thin or muscular. It's who you are as a person."[17]

Bulimia Nervosa

Bulimia nervosa is characterized by binge eating and purging. Binge eating is consuming large amounts of food in a short period of time (under two hours). This is followed by purging through vomiting, using laxatives and/or diuretics (substances that increase urine output), or excessive exercise. Bulimia nervosa affects both males and females. People with it tend to be "average weight, or fluctuate ten pounds above or below the normal weight for their height."[18] As a result, people with it may appear to be healthy. Symptoms of bulimia nervosa include: irregular menstrual periods, abdominal pain, lethargy, fatigue, headaches, depression, swelling of the hands and feet, and bloating.[19] Because people with bulimia nervosa often use vomiting as a method of purging, the enamel on their teeth can become eroded from repeated contact with stomach acid.

Binge Eating Disorder

Binge eating disorder, which is sometimes referred to as compulsive overeating, is a newly recognized disorder. Unlike those with bulimia nervosa, those with binge eating disorder do not purge. As a result, people with the disorder are often overweight. This disorder is not easily recognized. Some signs of binge eating disorder include: the inability to stop eating, eating unusually large amounts of food in a short period of time (under two hours), feeling guilty after eating, and feeling determined to stick to a diet or healthy eating after an eating episode.[20] In order to be considered binge eating disorder, the binges must average two or more times per week.[21]

Muscle Dysmorphia and Steroids

Muscle dysmorphia is a new area of study. It is not yet classified by the American Psychiatric Association as a disorder. Muscle dysmorphia is the belief that one's muscles are too small. It more commonly affects males, but females are affected as well.[22] Muscle dysmorphia is associated with other obsessive behaviors. Because people with it end up spending many hours in the gym trying to "bulk up," the disorder can interfere with personal relationships, school, and work. People who want larger muscles may resort to extreme measures, such as using steroids.[23]

Anabolic steroids are made from the male sex hormone, testosterone, and are often "taken for the purpose of increasing muscle size and strength."[24] The negative side effects far outweigh the gains. These side effects include increased blood pressure, decreased levels of HDL ("good") cholesterol, liver enzyme shrinkage, liver cancer, sterility, uncontrolled mood swings from depression to aggression, and testicle atrophy in males and breast shrinkage and uterus shrinkage in females.[25] In females, taking the male hormone can lead to facial hair and deepening of the voice. Long-term steroid use can lead to a breakdown of the joints, when muscle size becomes too large for the skeleton to support.

The psychological effects of steroids pose the biggest danger. When taking these drugs, some people experience extreme, violent mood swings, from mild irritability to severe aggressiveness. These changes in mood are often accompanied by impaired judgment and grandiose (exaggerated) beliefs.[26] Sudden bursts of aggression are known as "'roid rage."

Exercise Abuse

Exercise, when not overdone, can help to build confidence and maintain a healthy lifestyle. However, if abused, exercise can create problems. Exercise abuse may result from negative body feelings or from a fear of becoming overweight.

Symptoms of exercise abuse include constantly thinking of exercise, feeling anxiety when an exercise session is missed, continuing to exercise through injury, increasing exercise after overeating, and focusing on the amount of calories and fat burned while exercising.[27] Some studies show that exercise abuse can lead to eating disorders.[28] Similarly, people with eating disorders often abuse exercise as part of their efforts to reduce body fat and size.

In a Nutshell

Research and continued studies are showing the way to treatments and potential cures for body image disorders. It is known that body image problems can lead to very serious consequences, such as eating disorders and extreme behaviors to try to change one's body. Treatments need to address each individual's problem and may include both medication and behavior therapy.

3

The Price of Beauty: A Billion-Dollar Industry

No one person, group, or industry is totally responsible for the cultural idea that thin, in shape, and muscular equals the perfect body. For this "ideal" image to continue, people from all walks of life have to "buy into it." Americans spend billions of dollars every year on information that claims to provide quick fixes for body image problems, exercise equipment, diet pills, and cosmetics.

Over the past ten to twenty years, medical research showing the link between health and being thin and in shape has been distorted to create and perpetuate an "ideal" body image. While there are definite health risks with being overweight, some industries profit by perpetuating an idealized, unrealistic view of the perfect body.

Advertising—Tricks of the Trade

Advertisers often sell unrealistic promises using images of beauty. Ads seem to promise that any problem can be solved with a product. These claims might seem small when dealing with a shampoo, but when ads promise that a particular product can dramatically change body weight, muscle size, or breast size, then the claims become dangerous. By suggesting that products will make us feel fulfilled, advertising promotes an idea that our most important relationships are with the products we use.[1] Advertising changes the focus from people to products in order to solve problems.

While advertising itself does not cause problems, it does reinforce many cultural attitudes about the body. It is very rare to find a heavy woman in a television or magazine commercial, unless she is promoting a weight-loss product or a line of clothing for larger women. Heavier men can be found in commercials, but for the most part, men in advertising have muscular bodies with very low body fat. It is hard not to be affected by these images. Jean Kilbourne, who studies advertising, writes, "Because we think advertising is silly and trivial, we are less on guard, less critical, than we might otherwise be."[2]

Many people feel that advertising has no effect on them. However, advertisers believe differently. They spend over $200 billion a year.[3] An average television commercial costs $250,000 to make and another $250,000 to produce.[4] According to Kilbourne, "The average American is exposed to at least three thousand ads every day and will spend three years of his or her life watching television commercials."[5] It is easy to think of ads as the stuff placed in between favorite shows or in between articles in a magazine. By flipping to the next section of the magazine, the reader is forced to shuffle through pages of advertisements. "Advertising [pays for] more than 60 percent of magazine and newspaper production and almost 100 percent of the electronic media. Over $40 billion a year in ad [sales] revenue is [spent] for television and radio and over $30 billion for magazines and newspapers."[6]

DANGER SLIM

The Latest Diet Pills You'll Be Dying to Use!

Tired of exercising daily in an effort to lose your unwanted pounds? *Dangerslim* is the product for you. Need to lose weight quickly and safely in a short amount of time? Try *Dangerslim*. LOSE 10 POUNDS OR MORE IN A WEEK!

Fat Melts Away

When you take a *Dangerslim* pill, you'll feel the fat melting off you instantly. Not in a day, not in 6 hours, not even in 45 minutes—INSTANTLY!

Exercising and dieting take too long, but you will see the effects of *Dangerslim* right away. BE THE SIZE YOU WANT TO BE, without the exercise!

Lose Weight Safely

In our extensive laboratory studies* on the effects of *Dangerslim*, we've proven that *Dangerslim* is safe for most people.

IT'S TIME TO GET SLIM. Call now to order, and if you are not completely satisfied with our product, we'll send you a second order at a DISCOUNTED PRICE within ninety days.

Ask yourself this: Are you sick of sweating for hours under the hot lights of the gym? If so, then *Dangerslim* is the product for you! We'll help you LOSE WEIGHT QUICKLY with just one simple pill. What are you waiting for? Get to the phone now and order *Dangerslim*!

Eat All You Want . . . And Still Lose Weight!

*Studies done only on lab mice.

Advertisements like this made-up ad entice people by making it seem as if the product will change their lives or by promising unrealistic results.

In His Own Words

"I do not think guys are targeted the same way as girls in advertising, but I still want to look good." Mark, twelve years old, talks about his style. "I am involved in sports because it makes me feel better, both physically and mentally. Plus I learn sportsmanship and other skills. I also ski competitively. Having the right gear is important for racing, not just to do well, but to look good, too. I want to look cool on the slopes. We can tell just by looking who is a boy and who is a girl, even from far away. I would never wear pink, for example. That would not be cool. And I like to have the best gear."

"But I try not to feel pressured to look or dress a certain way," he goes on. "I want to look good for myself. Being yourself and finding your own style—*that* is cool."[7]

Right on Target—Special Market Advertising

To the advertiser, teens are the next generation of consumers. As young adults, teens have disposable income and broad interests. If a company or brand can "hook" a teen, then that company potentially has a lifelong buyer. If a company can convince a new consumer that its product is the best, why would the consumer shop around?

Many companies have partnerships with schools to create "educational" materials. "According to the Council for Aid to Education, the total amount corporations spend on 'educational' programs from kindergarten through high school has increased from $5 million in 1965 to about $500 million today." Companies support schools with money in exchange for vending machines placed in the school, and children learn to recognize corporate logos.[8] While schools definitely need money, the consumer must decide at what price.

Reality Bites—Food in Advertising

Advertising does not promote a realistic view of life. If reality is okay, then there is no need to buy a new product to make it better. Instead, advertisers show a world where life can be perfect if only a certain product is used. The ads sell a lifestyle and an image, not a realistic solution to a problem or need.

Think about the diet and junk food industries. If people were not overeating and gaining weight, there would be no need for diet (or fitness) products. Studies show, however, that restricting calories actually *slows* metabolism and puts the body into a reserve mode. When the body does not get the energy it needs (food), then it begins to hold on to all the reserve energy (fat) that it can. This creates a vicious and potentially dangerous cycle. Dieting has also been shown to cause intense food cravings and binges, causing physical and emotional pain. These feelings can lead a dieter to feel like a failure and advertisers have just the solution—food.

Advertisements routinely link food to emotional feelings and relationships. Kilbourne writes, "Food is intertwined with love throughout our culture. We give chocolates on Valentine's Day. We say that we are 'starved for affection.'"[9] One snack food offers the ultimate promise: "Feed your soul."[10]

The bottom line? A problem or perceived need must exist in order for the suppliers of products to exist. For example, if everyone felt good about his or her body size, the diet industry would not exist. This is not the case. Many people struggle with their body size and use methods that do not work, creating feelings of self-doubt and frustration. Food is often sold as a way to feel better. If dieting makes people feel bad, junk food will make them feel better—and then they can start dieting again. If those diet products actually worked, then the market for diet products would disappear, because everyone who used them would be thin. Advertisers need the consumer to return again and again. Otherwise, sales and profits would disappear along with the waistline.

Not Airheads—Airbrushed!

Models in magazines and advertisements look great—so great that one might wonder if it is realistic. It is not. For years photos in magazines have been altered. Airbrushing used to be a widely used technique, but now, with computer technology, changing photographs is easier than ever.

Magazine covers are designed to make a consumer buy the magazine. Fashion spreads make the clothing look as appealing as possible. If a model has a flaw, it can be easily removed. This is known as "helping the model."[11] Facial hair, wrinkles, blemishes, moles, shadows, and any other "flaws" are removed. Breasts are lifted or enlarged, teeth are whitened, eyes are brightened, and the body is adjusted.[12]

Young girls should strive to feel comfortable with their natural appearance and try not to compare themselves to models in magazines.

What does this mean? If a photograph looks too good to be real, it probably is. "In glamour and fashion magazines, the key is to portray subjects as attractively and alluringly as possible."[13] Even the models themselves cannot live up to the perfect image portrayed in the pictures.

The Cosmetics Industry— Commercialization at Its Best

The term "cosmetics" refers to "all preparations used externally to condition and beautify the body, by cleaning, coloring, softening, or protecting the skin, hair, nails, lips, or eyes."[14] Temporary tattoos and body painting kits are also considered cosmetics. But creams cannot melt away cellulite, and shampoo ads feature models who had their hair done by professional stylists. The shampoo did not create that fabulous look—the stylist did.

Companies actively target teens. In an article called "Girl Power!" about teen consumers and cosmetics, from the *Chemist and Druggist* journal, the author writes, "The youth market tends to be the prime target for cosmetic brands as these consumers are usually more experimental in their choice of brands, products and shades. They also tend to be heavy users, making them a highly [profitable group]."[15]

Cosmetics are not targeted just to girls. Colognes, deodorants, soaps, shampoos, and more are also geared toward boys. There is nothing wrong with wanting to smell nice and look good. But keep in mind that the cosmetics industry is not concerned about that—they want people, teens in particular, to buy their products.

Buyer Beware—Weight-Loss Scams

Weight-loss and exercise equipment scams promising to melt away pounds and burn off inches can be found everywhere. Turn on the television, and chances are good that some sort of weight-loss advertisement will come on. Magazines are filled with such ads. If ads for these products make claims that sound too good to be true, they are. Exercising for only three minutes a day will not completely reshape someone's body. Nor will attaching electronic wires to the body result in larger muscles.

Weight-loss products are just as misleading. Taking a pill does not lead to health and fitness. Many of the pills and creams on the market can be dangerous, and none of these products is regulated by the Food and Drug Administration.

In a Nutshell

Advertisers want their products to seem irresistible. But what is shown in commercials and ads is not always real. By keeping a level head and remembering this, shoppers can determine what they want and need.

4

Maintaining a Healthy Body Image in Everyday Life

It is perfectly normal to want to look and feel good. Activities such as exercising, healthy eating, and having fun all contribute to this. Special attention and outside help need to be considered when these activities are taken to an extreme, such as severely limiting food intake, overexercising, or using dangerous drugs.

Healthy Exercise

Exercise takes many shapes and forms. Playing a game of volleyball can provide a great aerobic workout as well as fun. Certain sports, such as gymnastics, provide a strength workout from the moves performed. The important thing to remember is to do an activity that is enjoyable.

Exercise has many positive mental and emotional benefits. Aerobic exercise, which increases heart rate and breathing, keeps the heart healthy. Weight training keeps muscles and the skeletal system strong. A well-rounded exercise program includes aerobic, weight, and flexibility training.

Make It Fun!

Exercise should be fun. A night out dancing can provide a great aerobic workout, as well as a chance to hang out with friends. If the exercise is not fun, chances are much greater that it will be skipped—and that can lead to feelings of guilt or lower self-esteem. Having someone to exercise with can also be a great help. Find a workout partner or group of friends who enjoys the same types of activities and start moving together.

In Her Own Words

Jennifer, twelve, is a middle-school student. "In gym class, we're working on learning healthy eating and exercise habits. I know this is the time to develop good habits because if I don't, it will show when I am an adult. I don't try and watch what I eat, but I don't eat too much. I can't make it through the day without food. My brain doesn't function if I don't eat. I play soccer because it's fun and I like it. The side benefits are that it helps me feel good about myself and it's good exercise.

"I think that doing exercise that is activity-based is a good idea, because then it doesn't feel like exercise—like soccer, biking or hiking. I can't imagine sitting on an exercise bike for a long period of time. But a bike ride outside is fun." One of Jennifer's assignments in school is to develop an eating and exercise plan. "I think it will be helpful. If it's something I design myself, I'm more likely to follow it because it will be things that I enjoy."[1]

Healthy Nutrition

The U.S. Department of Agriculture's (USDA) Food Guide Pyramid is an excellent nutrition resource. The Pyramid sorts food into six categories. While it suggests servings, these are only guidelines. Serving sizes, both in the Pyramid guidelines and especially on packaging labels, are often much smaller than expected. How much is too much or too little? The best way to know is to learn to recognize the body's signs of hunger and fullness.

A 1991 study from *The New England Journal of Medicine* showed that when young children are allowed to decide what and how much to eat, they end up eating a healthy and balanced range of foods over several days.[2] However, researchers Jennifer O. Fisher and Leann L. Birch cite a study showing that most children aged two to nineteen are not getting adequate nutrition. Developing healthy habits includes eating a variety of healthy foods but not eliminating any one food group; everything is okay in moderation.

High-protein diets are often popular because people who use them tend to lose weight. However, eating too much protein and eliminating many fruits and vegetables can be very unhealthy. Following this type of diet increases risk for

Exercising does not have to be work—it can be a fun activity with friends.

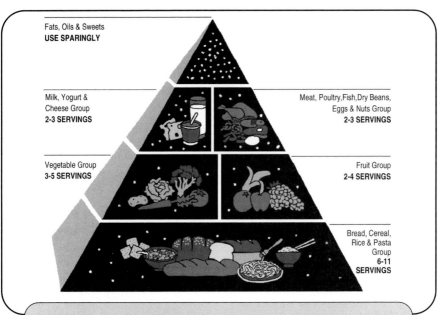

Fats, Oils & Sweets
USE SPARINGLY

Milk, Yogurt &
Cheese Group
2-3 SERVINGS

Meat, Poultry,Fish,Dry Beans,
Eggs & Nuts Group
2-3 SERVINGS

Vegetable Group
3-5 SERVINGS

Fruit Group
2-4 SERVINGS

Bread, Cereal,
Rice & Pasta
Group
**6-11
SERVINGS**

Following the Food Guide Pyramid is an excellent way to make sure you eat right.

heart disease and cancer.[3] It is also low in calcium, which is unhealthy for growing bones. Following the Food Guide Pyramid and listening to body signals can lead to an intake of many foods, and therefore meeting nutritional needs.

Supplements

The U.S. Congress defined a supplement as "a product taken by mouth that contains a 'dietary ingredient' intended to supplement the diet . . . including vitamins, minerals, herbs or other botanicals, amino acids, and substances such as enzymes, organ tissues, glandulars, and metabolites."[4] Very few people need supplements, except for those with specific nutritional or medical problems.[5]

Many products make claims about improving health or athletic performance, and there is no government regulation for these supplements.[6] "The dietary supplement manufacturer is responsible for ensuring that a dietary supplement is safe before it is marketed. The FDA is responsible for taking action against any unsafe dietary supplement product after it reaches the market."[7] Supplements can be dangerous. Ephedrine, an herbal stimulant common in "fat burning" products, can cause "high blood pressure, racing heartbeat, insomnia, and sometimes severe cardiovascular complications."[8]

Just because a product comes from a plant or says it is "natural" does not mean it is good for you. As nutritionist Wendy Nelson put it, "Snake venom is natural."[9]

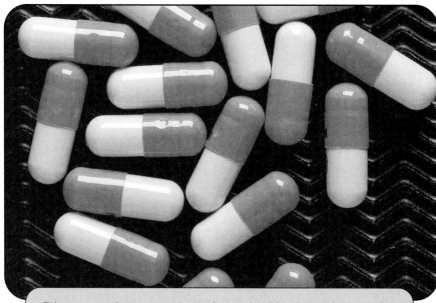

Dietary supplements are not always healthy for teens, and they are only regulated by the government after they have been made available to the public.

Charts and Genetics

Height/weight charts, which show "ideal" weight for people according to their height, might be helpful in providing general guidelines. However, these charts do not take into consideration a person's genetics or body composition. Weight measures everything, including muscle, fat, and water. For example, muscle weighs more than fat. Body composition is the ratio of body fat to fat-free body mass. Body fat is related to overall health, and therefore body composition is a better indication of health than weight alone. A person might look thin but be very unhealthy due to a high level of body fat.

Taking Action

"When I was in seventh grade, we had to do body fat testing in school," explains Shauna, now a senior in high school. "It was very embarrassing. The teacher did the skin caliper method, where you pinch fat on various parts of the body and measure it. She did this in the back of the classroom, where anyone could turn around and look. After we calculated the results, we had to call out our body fat percentage in front of the whole class. I was heavier then, and the teacher made rude comments about those of us who had a higher percentage. It was really degrading. I had never really thought of myself as overweight before then, but I did after that. I know that it was also very hard on some other students.

"I don't usually get mad, but this really got me upset. So I decided to do something about it. I started a petition against body fat testing in school, and got all the students to sign it. The teacher said the testing was part of the curriculum, but students in the other middle schools didn't have to do it. So I got it stopped in my school. Seventh grade was tough enough without having to go through that humiliation.

"I definitely felt better after doing the petition. It gave me some control over the situation, and helped my self-confidence. And now, other students don't have to go through that. As far as I know, body fat testing in the middle school has been stopped. The body is just going through too many changes at that age to worry about body fat. Now that I'm older, my body and metabolism have stabled, and I feel much better about myself."[10]

Self-Expression

These days, in popular American culture, clothing, hairstyles and hair color, cosmetics, jewelry, body paint, piercing, and tattooing are all common methods for self-expression.

The availability and ease of hair coloring makes it easy to change from one week to the next, if desired. Using clothing, jewelry, and cosmetics to accent a look are easy ways to define a style. Sean's story in Chapter 1 shows that it is possible to have a very unique style without changing actual physical appearance. He does not dye his hair, has no tattoos, and except for his ears, has no piercings. Yet his style is definitely unique.

Piercing and tattooing are quite popular. There are some definite risks, including infection and diseases such as hepatitis and HIV. *All piercings and tattoos should be done by a professional.* Professionals have autoclaves, which are necessary to sanitize needles and jewelry, and they also have the required experience and training. Anyone doing a piercing or tattoo should wear new rubber gloves and use new needles. In addition, using proper jewelry is very important for piercings. And except for earlobes, no piercing should be done with an ear-piercing gun. For legal and safety reasons, many professionals will not pierce or tattoo anyone under eighteen years of age.

Taking the time to wait and make a firm decision to be pierced or tattooed can be worth it. While piercing is not permanent, it can leave scars. And for the most part, a tattoo is something a person will live with for the rest of his or her life.

Laser and removal techniques are available, but they are expensive. These techniques can be very painful, may leave scars, and may not always completely remove the tattoo.[11] If a tattoo or piercing is desired, take time to talk with the professional beforehand to ask questions. Also make sure that the person has experience and some type of formal training. Talk to other clients to find out if they are satisfied with their results.

Words of Experience

Josie, nineteen, has two tattoos and two piercings. "I pierced my tongue to be rebellious, and I had always wanted my belly button done. So when I turned eighteen, I got them done. My tattoos, however, are very personal. I have a scorpion on my shoulder because I am a Scorpio, and I always will be. So I don't think I will ever regret it. I also thought about it for a long time before I had it done. I think that anyone who wants to get a tattoo should pick a design and then think about it for a year. If you still want it after that long, then you probably won't regret it.

"The other tattoo I have is of a rose. It's dedicated to my

A popular method of self-expression is through body piercing. Body piercing carries risks, however, which should be investigated before proceeding.

best friend from high school. We always said we would have it done, and she is a true friend.

"I am planning on having another tattoo done. My sister is designing it. This one will be of a horse. I love horses, and always have. And because my sister is designing it, it will also be very personal.

"I have tattoos and piercings to express who I am. I had them all done by the same person, who is very professional and clean. And I take very good care of them. I cleaned the piercings as directed, and as for the tattoos, I don't go out into the sun and I use lotion. Good care makes a big difference."[12]

When Does Body Image Get in the Way?

Body image concerns become problems when they begin interfering with everyday life. If a person spends a lot of time thinking or obsessing about his or her looks, then that is a definite warning sign. Lots of time spent in the gym at the expense of other activities is a sign of a problem. Refusing to eat or spending lots of time in the bathroom following meals can also be a sign of a more serious issue.

Talk About It

When faced with someone who might have a body image or eating disorder problem, it is hard to know what to do. The first step is to talk to the person. While this can be a difficult discussion to have, it is important to remember that the person's health is the main concern. Talking to the person may influence his or her recovery. The authors of *Surviving an Eating Disorder* suggest the following guidelines when speaking with someone. These guidelines can also be applied to a talk about any body image concern.

1. Think through who is the best person to do the talking. It may be a friend, sibling, or parent. If the person you are concerned about is under

eighteen years of age, talk to him or her before going to an authority, but do get outside help.

2. Pick a time to talk when feeling calm. Angry or upset feelings may make it hard for the person to open up.

3. Pick a time to talk when the conversation will not be interrupted. Talking a few minutes before a class or other scheduled activity will not be enough time.

4. Consider writing down what will be said ahead of time. This can help keep the conversation on track.

Before talking, think about why the conversation is needed, what feelings led to the conversation, and what the goals are. It may be helpful to let the person know that his or her friends are worried and want to seek help. Listing behaviors that have been noticed can show why there is concern. Also let him or her know that professional help is being sought and why. If the conversation gets out of control, stop and walk away. It is better to continue later, when emotions are not running out of control.

Sometimes a person will feel relieved after being approached by friends. After hiding a problem, it may be a relief to be "discovered" and move on to getting help. Other times, the person may deny there is a problem. When this happens, the best solution is to contact a professional for a consultation. This could be an eating disorder center or specialist, a peer support group, a hot line, a school counselor, or a member of the clergy. When meeting with a professional, have a list of concerns, behaviors that have been noticed, and what has been done so far. The suspected person's health and well-being is the top priority.[13] Keep in mind that a person may show some of the warning signs but not have a disorder. Similarly, someone with a disorder may not exhibit all of the

Anorexia Nervosa Warning Signs

- People see themselves as much fatter than they actually are
- Rapid and/or severe weight loss
- Excessive concern with weight and appearance
- Extreme fear of gaining weight
- Compulsive exercise
- Refusal to keep body weight at or above 85 percent of normal weight
- Loss of menstrual period
- Unable to see body size for what it really is; denial of low body weight[14]

Bulimia Nervosa Warning Signs

- Eating large amounts of food in a short period of time (two hours or less)
- Purging through vomiting, laxatives, or diuretics to control weight
- Feeling out of control when eating
- Bingeing and purging behaviors occur at least twice a week for three months or more (on average)
- Loss of menstrual period
- Self-esteem heavily influenced by body shape and weight[15]

Binge Eating Warning Signs

- Eating large amounts of food in a short period of time (two hours or less)
- Feeling out of control when eating
- At least three of the following:
  1. Eating very fast
  2. Eating until full or uncomfortably full
  3. Eating large amounts of food when not physically hungry
  4. Eating alone out of embarrassment
  5. Feeling disgusted or guilty after eating
- Feeling upset about the binges
- The binges occur at least two times per week for six months (on average)
- Binge eating does not include other forms of purging, fasting, or excessive exercise associated with anorexia or bulimia[16]

Body Dysmorphic Disorder Warning Signs

- Preoccupation with a slight or imagined defect in appearance
- Preoccupation causes severe distress and/or interferes with social life, work life, or other important areas of functioning
- Preoccupation does not fit symptoms of another disorder such as anorexia[17]

Muscle Dysmorphia Warning Signs

- Preoccupation with muscle size
- Long hours in the gym lifting weights and special attention to diet
- Two or more of the following:
  1. Frequently giving up social, work, or recreational activities to keep up with workout and/or diet schedule
  2. Avoiding situations where the body is exposed to other people or becoming very stressed in these situations
  3. Preoccupation with muscle size interferes with social, work, and other areas of functioning
  4. Continuing to work out, diet, or use performance-enhancing substances even if it interferes with emotional or physical health
  5. Primary focus is on muscle size (too small), as opposed to other types of body dissatisfaction[18]

Steroid Use Warning Signs

- Rapid weight gain
- Excessive musculature, particularly in the shoulders and neck
- "Hypermale" look; muscle size is out of proportion compared to what can be achieved naturally
- Sudden changes in mood; irritability, violent outbreaks, "'roid rage"
- Depression, particularly when coming off the drug[19]

warning signs. Only a professional can diagnose a disorder or serious problem.

The Facts

Exercising a specific part of the body will not ensure fat loss from that area. Training specific muscles can change their size, but will not change the amount of fat covering them.

A well-balanced combination of healthy eating and exercise is the best way to maintain a healthy weight. Diet pills can be very dangerous and surgical procedures for weight loss are usually reserved for severely obese individuals. Diets do not work. If they did, there would not be a need for new ones. Similarly, special clothing and tight clothing or body wraps that do not allow sweat to evaporate can be very dangerous and should be avoided.[20]

In a Nutshell

No one can escape the genes he or she is born with, which affect how a person looks. However, our culture places enormous pressure on looking one particular way—a way that only very few people are able to obtain. Balancing a healthy exercise program with informed eating choices and taking part in enjoyable, athletic activities can help a person maintain a healthy body image.

5

Treatments and Prevention

Some body image disorders can be hard to diagnose, such as muscle dysmorphia and bulimia nervosa. Those who have these problems often do not want to admit it, especially boys. Men are taught that to have these types of problems is being "girly," and they are often embarrassed to speak out. For those who have body image problems, the important thing to remember is that they are not alone, regardless of gender. It is also important to remember that many people suffer some degree of body dissatisfaction. While the disorders presented below are often not diagnosed until the problem has become severe, many people suffer to a lesser degree. Talking about these issues and increasing awareness and education may be one key to keeping many people from reaching advanced stages of dissatisfaction. As the authors of *The Adonis Complex* write, "Secrecy and embarrassment are the single greatest impediment to getting help."[1]

How Are Body Image Problems Diagnosed?

Body dysmorphic disorder can be hard to diagnose, mostly because of the shame and embarrassment associated with it. People who suffer from it may feel that they are overly vain. Relationships may have failed because of the person's preoccupation with the imagined defect or from spending time dealing with the defect instead of with friends and family. When a person with body dysmorphic disorder asks someone if he or she looks okay, the response is usually that the person looks fine. The sufferer may feel that this response is given either out of sympathy or dishonesty, when in fact, the person being questioned honestly cannot see the problem.

Over the past twenty years or so, body dysmorphic disorder has gained recognition. But it still remains a mystery to many people, even though a large part of the population suffers from some type of it. While this disorder seems like a physical problem, it is a mental health issue, because the person constantly thinks about the imagined defect.

The best thing a person with body dysmorphic disorder can do is to seek a qualified mental health professional, preferably someone who has experience with body image issues. Many people with the disorder seek surgical solutions first and often feel that the surgery made the condition worse. Instead of seeking a mental health professional, a person with body dysmorphic disorder will often seek out more and more surgery. However, combinations of certain medications for depression and serotonin levels, combined with behavioral therapy that works to change a person's actions, have been shown to be highly effective in treating body dysmorphic disorder.

Similarly, diagnosing muscle dysmorphia can be hard, both because it is difficult for those who have it to come forward, and also because this is a newly recognized problem. Muscle dysmorphia usually affects men, but can affect women as well. Spending time in the gym and caring about one's weight are looked upon as healthy activities, and often they are. But when those activities become obsessive, it is time to take a closer look.

One of the biggest hurdles in diagnosing muscle dysmorphia is a person's insecurity about appearing vain and feeling like he or she is the "only one" with this problem. In the United States, the number of men with severe muscle dysmorphia might be as high as one hundred thousand.[2] This number does not include those who suffer from signs of muscle dysmorphia to a lesser degree. People who suffer from it and those close to them may realize there is a problem, but not know what to call it. Having the courage to come forward may be difficult, but knowing that it is a common problem might ease the pain for all those involved.

Eating disorders may be easier to diagnose because of the physical signs. They can affect both males and females. Being aware of the warning signs can help to pinpoint the problem.

A person with anorexia nervosa is usually very thin. The person has an intense fear of gaining weight and feels fat even with weight loss. A person with anorexia nervosa will usually lose weight through starvation but may also use bingeing or exercise to accelerate weight loss.

Those with bulimia nervosa and binge eating disorder may be harder to diagnose through physical appearance. A person with bulimia nervosa cannot be diagnosed by weight, because the person will engage in both bingeing and purging. After eating large amounts of food, the bulimic will then purge through vomiting, laxatives, or excessive exercise. Disapproving thoughts of oneself often follow the binges.

Binge eating disorder is probably the hardest to diagnose of the eating disorders, because of the shame involved. People with the disorder are often embarrassed about their binges, as they are usually in control of all other areas of their lives. As a result, they try to hide their behavior. Although the person's body weight is not an accurate tool to determine a problem, those with binge eating disorder are often overweight because purging does not follow the binges. Additionally, someone with binge eating disorder is generally aware that the eating pattern is abnormal. As with bulimia nervosa, disapproving thoughts of oneself often follow the binges.[3] But because more research and attention have been given to eating disorders, it may be easier for friends and family to spot the disease before it becomes a physical danger.

Current Treatments for Body Dysmorphic Disorder

Body dysmorphic disorder is best treated with a combination of therapy and medication. Cognitive-behavioral therapy focuses on a person's thoughts, emotions, and behaviors. Through therapy, a person studies the negative thoughts and behaviors associated with the problem and learns more effective ways to cope. This type of therapy addresses the idea that a person has developed thought patterns that are unhealthy.

Certain medications that affect chemicals in the brain can support cognitive-behavioral therapy. Serotonin is a chemical in the brain that affects moods. One type of medication, called serotonin-reuptake inhibitors, has been shown to be effective in treating body dysmorphic disorder, because they also reduce obsessive thoughts that are part of it.[4] One of the most promising medications is *Clomipramine*, also known as Anafranil, which is an antidepressant used in obsessive disorders.[5]

Current Treatments for Muscle Dysmorphia

Muscle dysmorphia is similar to body dysmorphic disorder in that a person focuses on a particular body part. However, while body dysmorphic disorder can focus on any body part, muscle dysmorphia is always about muscle size. Because muscle dysmorphia is a newly recognized condition, very few studies have been done on treatments. However, researchers who have worked with many muscle dysmorphia patients have found that effective treatment is similar to that for body dysmorphic disorder. Cognitive-behavioral therapy, which works with both a person's thinking and behavioral patterns, is recommended, possibly along with medication. These researchers found that in some cases, certain antidepressant medications that are effective in treating obsessive-compulsive disorders are also effective in treating muscle dysmorphia.[6]

Current Treatments for Anorexia Nervosa and Bulimia Nervosa

For severe cases of anorexia, a hospital stay is necessary to ensure the health of the patient. After that, treatment may include individual, group, and family therapy. The patient also learns nutritional and health-related information to aid the healing process. A combination of education and treatment is best, including work with a physician, counselor, and nutritionist. Family therapy is especially important so that those closest to the person become aware of warning signs and food attitudes that may be present in the household, such as a parent's own fears of gaining weight.

Eating disorders are not about food. They are about how a person thinks and feels about his or her body. The goal of treatment is to get to the root of the problem. Some treatments include educating the person about the physical results of restricted eating, such as bone loss, hair loss, lack of concentration, problems with the heart muscle, and even death.[7] Treatment also includes learning about healthy nutrition and, eventually, how to listen to and trust the body's hunger signals.[8] Other factors may be examined, such as friends, family, and body image issues. Working toward healthy self-esteem will help the person regain and maintain a healthy body weight.

As with anorexia nervosa, bulimia nervosa treatment also focuses on education, counseling, and seeing a physician. Physical side effects specifically related to bulimia nervosa include damage to the esophagus and teeth from vomiting and problems with the intestinal system from using laxatives.[9] In some cases, surgery may be needed to fix the bowels.[10] Severe cases of bulima nervosa can lead to death. Studies show that antidepressants can be very helpful for those suffering from bulima nervosa.[11] Possible medications include Paxil, Zoloft or Prozac, Luvox, and Celexa.[12] These antidepressants also help the brain utilize serotonin. "Depletion of serotonin is associated with cravings to binge or purge, as well as depression."[13]

Cognitive-behavioral therapy is likely to be used to help treat either of these eating disorders. This may include examining a person's beliefs and attitudes toward food, promoting healthy attitudes and educating about correct nutritional information.

Current Treatments for Binge Eating Disorder

Cognitive-behavioral therapy may also play an important role in treating binge eating disorder. Learning to develop healthy attitudes toward food and learning to trust the body's signals may be a part of therapy. Learning to deal with emotions through counseling can help a person with binge eating disorder. As with bulimia nervosa, some antidepressants may help the person deal with the compulsive aspect of the disorder.

Help for Steroid Abuse

A person using steroids will probably not want anyone to know about it. Also, he or she will probably not want to stop using the steriods. Perhaps the best help for steroid abuse is knowledge. Awareness that many of the images presented in the movies, media and advertising are of men who could only have reached that level of muscularity by using illegal drugs may help men realize that these images are not realistic. These images are not natural and can come at a high price, both in psychological side effects and long-term health problems. Steroid use may become less of a problem as our culture learns that these images of men are not natural.

When Is Surgery Appropriate?

Surgical procedures to deal with body image issues should be seriously considered before taking action. For those with body dysmorphic disorder, even after surgery the person may feel that the problem has not been corrected or has gotten

In Her Own Words

"I think it's hard not to feel pressure to look a certain way. It's easy to feel self-conscious. We see all these famous people and pictures in magazines, and want to look like them.

"I feel pretty good about how I look, but I didn't always. It's hard to get past that. It's really hard to get over it. I have to remind myself that it's okay to be unique, and I try not to copy the trends.

"I've also gotten involved in sports. I swim and do kick boxing. It helps me feel more confident physically. And it's fun.

"It's also important to focus on other things. You have to stop being so self-absorbed. You need to get out of yourself. I teach at a tennis camp, and that's a lot of fun.

"I would like to see more positive stories about others. We only hear about the negative stories, but it's important to know that some of us are doing okay. Yeah, it's hard, but I like to think it's getting better. I want to have hope."[14]

—Rebecca, age 14

worse. Josleen Wilson, author of *The American Society of Plastic and Reconstructive Surgeons' Guide to Cosmetic Surgery*, writes, "Experienced plastic surgeons usually can spot someone whose desire for surgery is deeply rooted in a longstanding psychiatric condition and such a person usually will not be accepted for surgery."[15] The body is still developing and growing into the late teens and early twenties; because of this, surgical decisions need to be seriously considered and discussed with a qualified, experienced surgeon. "Good plastic surgeons understand the need for personal, hands-on care throughout the process."[16] A candidate for plastic surgery should make sure the physician is certified by the American Society of Plastic and Reconstructive Surgeons and get a second opinion.

Steps to a Positive Body Image—Prevention

Many things can be done to develop and maintain a positive body image. Self-esteem is not determined by appearance alone. Developing special talents contributes to positive self-esteem, which helps maintain a positive body image. Developing healthy attitudes toward food and exercise helps. Exercise keeps a body healthy, and is a healthy way to blow off steam and deal with stress. Also, participating in enjoyable sports can add to a healthy attitude about the body. Sports keep the body strong and healthy, and promote teamwork and self-confidence.

Carrying oneself in a positive way also promotes a positive body image. Standing tall and making eye contact with others shows self-confidence. Keeping an open, relaxed stance shows friendliness and self-acceptance. Also, being surrounded with positive people makes it easier to feel good.

Self-expression, which includes everything from creative writing to drawing to dancing, shows uniqueness. Even if these things are not shared with others, self-expression can

Working together to help others can build confidence—and take your mind off yourself.

help a person deal with feelings in a positive way. Dealing with emotions, rather than stuffing them inside, helps keep things in perspective. It is also okay to seek outside help to deal with emotions and problems.

Remember that the body is an amazing machine. Instead of wasting energy focusing on the negatives, think about all the amazing things the body does without any conscious thought. Learn to appreciate the body for all it does.

Volunteering to help others can help take the focus off personal problems, including negative thoughts about food and body image. And most importantly, if someone is showing any warning signs of having a problem, talk to the person immediately and get help.

Finally, focus on the positives. Look for beauty in others, both inside and out. And look for beauty in the world.[17]

In a Nutshell

In the most extreme forms, body image problems can lead to a variety of disorders. And for all those who suffer from these disorders, there are many more people who suffer to a less extreme degree. Body image disturbance is so common in our society that it seems universal. "Dieting, exercising, fasting, and a preoccupation with food and weight are so much a part of our culture that it is unusual to find a [teenager or adult] who is not or has not been concerned with weight."[19] Advice can be found everywhere on how to "look good to attract a mate," "lose ten pounds over the weekend," or "dress for success." It is hard not to be taken in by so many messages. Even daily conversations often turn to having a "bad hair

Other Things to Do

- Keep a list of things you like about yourself.
- If you have body image concerns, remember: You're not alone. Find someone to talk to about it.
- Keep a journal.
- Trust your body. It knows what it needs.
- Express yourself. Do something creative.
- Listen to your body. Pay attention to the hunger and fullness signals. Are you eating because you are bored or sad or because your body needs nourishment? Learning to recognize the signals can help maintain a positive relationship with food.
- Remember that it is okay to be yourself.[18]

A good group of supportive friends can help teens deal with pressure in a positive way.

day," or "eating bad." It is hard not to feel the pressure, or at least notice how common these thoughts and conversations are. But by taking active preventive measures, this trend might shift. Talking about these issues and staying educated are important steps towards keeping a positive and healthy body image.

Every Body Is Unique

Each person has physical and personality traits that make him or her a unique individual. Rates of development and genetic makeup differ from person to person. These differences are often portrayed as out of the ordinary or even "bad," when in fact very few people live up to the cultural ideal of the "perfect" body and look. By not giving in to the pressure to look a certain way and embracing the differences, body image problems may become less and less common.

Chapter Notes

Chapter 1. What Is Body Image?

1. Personal Interview with Sean (real name withheld for privacy), October 5, 2001.

2. Bobby Guinn, et. al., "Body image perception in female Mexican-American adolescents," *Journal of School Health*, March 1997, vol. 67, no. 3, p. 112: Randy M. Page and Tanya S. Page, *Fostering Emotional Well-Being in the Classroom* (Boston, Mass.: Jones and Bartlett Publishers, 1993), pp. RM, TS.

3. Lynn Meskell, "Goddesses, Gimbutas and 'New Age' archaeology," *Antiquity*, March 1995, vol. 69, no. 262, p. 74.

4. Terry Poulton, *No Fat Chicks: How Big Business Profits by Making Women Hate Their Bodies—and How to Fight Back* (Secaucus, N.J.: A Birch Lane Press Book Published by Carol Publishing Group, 1997), p. 12.

5. Ibid.

6. Kare Anderson, "Creating a positive first impression," *Nursing*, March 1998, vol. 28, no. 3, p. 60.

7. Leslie J. Heinberg, "Theories of Body Image Disturbance," *Body Image, Eating Disorders, and Obesity: An Integrative Guide for Assessment and Treatment*, J. Kevin Thompson, ed. (Washington, D.C.: American Psychological Association, 1996), p. 30.

8. Ibid.

9. Jennifer A. O'Dea and Suzanne Abraham, "Association between self-concept and body weight, gender, and pubertal development among male and female adolescents," *Adolescence*, Spring 1999, vol. 34, issue 133, p. 69.

10. Michele Siegel, Ph.D., Judith Brisman, Ph.D., and Margot Weinshel, M.S.W., *Surviving an Eating Disorder: Strategies for Family and Friends, Revised and Updated* (New York: HarperPerennial, 1997 (1988)), pp. 61–62.

11. Harrison G. Pope, Jr., MD, Katherine A. Phillips, MD, and Roberto Olivardia, Ph.D., *The Adonis Complex: The Secret Crisis of Male Body Obsession* (New York: The Free Press, 2000), p. 73.

12. Beth L. Molloy and Sharon D. Herzberger, "Body image and self-esteem: a comparison of African-American and Caucasian women," *Sex Roles: A Journal of Research*, April 1998, vol. 38, no. 7–8, p. 631–643.

13. Guinn, et. al., p. 4.

Chapter 2. Body Image Disturbances

1. J. Kevin Thompson, ed., *Body Image, Eating Disorders, and Obesity: An Integrative Guide for Assessment and Treatment* (Washington, D.C.: American Psychological Association, 1996), p. 28.

2. Leslie J. Heinberg, "Theories of Body Image Disturbance," *Body Image, Eating Disorders, and Obesity: An Integrative Guide for Assessment and Treatment*, J. Kevin Thompson, ed. (Washington, D.C.: American Psychological Association, 1996), p. 29.

3. Ibid., p. 31.

4. Ibid.

5. Ibid., pp. 37–38.

6. Jeffrey T. Kirchner, D.O., "Treatment of Patients with Body Dysmorphic Disorder," *American Family Physician*, March 15, 2000, vol. 61, no. 6, p. 1,837.

7. Bruce Bower, "Deceptive Appearances: Imagined Physical Defects Take an Ugly Personal Toll," *Science News*, July 15, 1995, vol. 148, pp. 40–41.

8. Katherine Phillips, et. al., "Case study: body Dysmorphic disorder in adolescents," *Journal of the American Academy of Child and Adolescent Psychiatry*, September 1995, vol. 34, no. 9, p. 1,216.

9. Thompson, p. 153.

10. Bower, p. 40.

11. Ibid.

12. Harrison G. Pope, Jr., MD, Katherine A. Phillips, MD, and Roberto Olivardia, Ph.D., *The Adonis Complex: The Secret Crisis of Male Body Obsession* (New York: The Free Press, 2000), pp. 158–161.

13. Glen D. Morgan, "Health Behaviors Psychology," *Lifestyle and Weight Management Consultant Manual*, Richard T. Cotton, ed. (San Diego, Calif.: American Council on Exercise, 1996), p. 38.

14. Susan J. Bartlett, Ross E. Anderson, and Lawrence J. Cheskin, "Screening, Assessment and Referral," *Lifestyle and Weight Management Consultant Manual*, Richard T. Cotton, ed. (San Diego, Calif.: American Council on Exercise, 1996), pp. 131–132.

15. Marian B. Tanofsky and Denise E. Wilfley, "The Psychology of Weight Management and Obesity," *Lifestyle and Weight Management Consultant Manual*, Richard T. Cotton, ed. (San Diego, Calif.: American Council on Exercise, 1996), p. 65.

16. Ibid.

17. Personal interview with Daniel (real name withheld for privacy), October 25, 2001.

18. Tanofsky, p. 66.

19. Ibid., p. 65.

20. Ibid., p. 66.

21. Lawrence J. Cheskin, "Special Populations," *Lifestyle and Weight Management Consultant Manual*, Richard T. Cotton, ed. (San Diego, Calif.: American Council on Exercise, 1996), p. 256.

22. Burkhard Bilger, "Barbell blues (bodybuilders with 'muscle dysmorphia' see themselves as too small)," *The Sciences*, January–February 1998, vol. 38, no. 1, p. 10.

23. Pope, Phillips, Olivardia, pp. 88, 92.

24. Wayne L. Westcott, "Muscular Strength and Endurance," *Personal Trainer Manual: The Resource for Fitness Instructors*, Mitchell Sudy, ed. (San Diego, Calif.: American Council on Exercise, 1991), p. 247.

25. Ibid.

26. Pope, Phillips, Olivardia, p. 111.

27. Tanofsky, p. 66.

28. Caroline Davis, "Body Image, Exercise, and Eating Disorders," *The Physical Self: From Motivation to Well-Being*, Kenneth R. Fox, Ph.D., ed. (Champaign, Ill.: University of Exetor, 1997), p. 164.

Chapter 3. The Price of Beauty:
A Billion-Dollar Industry

1. Jean Kilbourne, *Deadly Persuasion: Why Women and Girls Must Fight the Addictive Power of Advertising* (New York: The Free Press, 1999), pp. 81–89.

2. Ibid., p. 27.

3. Ibid., p. 33.

4. Ibid., pp. 33–34.

5. Ibid., p. 58.

6. Ibid., pp. 34–35.

7. Personal interview with Mark (real name withheld for privacy), March 20, 2001.

8. Kilbourne, p. 46.

9. Ibid., p. 109.

10. 2001 Nabisco, Inc., advertisement for Corn Nuts snacks.

11. Dino A Brugioni, *Photo Fakery: The History and Techniques of Photographic Deception and Manipulation* (Dulles, Va.: Brassey's, 1999), p. 15.

12. Ibid.

13. Ibid.

14. "Cosmetics," Microsoft Encarta Reference Suite, 2001.

15. "Girl Power! (Marketing Cosmetics and Toiletries to Adolescent Women)," *Chemist & Druggist*, October 14, 2000, p. 19.

Chapter 4. Maintaining a Healthy Body Image in Everyday Life

1. Personal interview with Jennifer (real name withheld for privacy), October 28, 2001.

2. Jane R. Hirschmann, C.S.W., and Lela Zaphiropoulos, C.S.W., *Preventing Childhood Eating Problems* (Carlsbad, Calif.: Gürze Books, 1993, 1985), p. x.

3. Personal interview with Wendy Nelson, registered dietitian, March 27, 2001.

4. U.S. Food and Drug Administration, n.d., "Overview of Dietary Supplements," n.d., <http://vm.cfsan.fda.gov/~dms/ds-overview.html #what> (November 2, 2001).

5. Personal interview with Wendy Nelson.

6. Ibid.

7. U.S. Food and Drug Administration, "Dietary Supplements," n.d., <http://www.cfsan.fda.gov/~dms/supplmnt.html> (November 2, 2001).

8. Harrison G. Pope, Jr., MD, Katherine A. Phillips, MD, and Roberto Olivardia, Ph.D., *The Adonis Complex: The Secret Crisis of Male Body Obsession* (New York: The Free Press, 2000), p. 120.

9. Personal interview with Wendy Nelson.

10. Personal interview with Shauna (real name withheld for privacy), October 25, 2001.

11. U.S. Food and Drug Administration, Center for Food Safety and Applied Nutrition, Office of Cosmetics and Colors Fact Sheet, "Tattoos and Permanent Makeup," November 29, 2001, <http://www.cfsan. fda.gov/~dms/cos-204.html> (November 2, 2001).

12. Personal interview with Josie (real name withheld for privacy), October 2, 2001.

13. Michele Siegel, Ph.D., Judith Brisman, Ph.D., and Margot Weinshel, M.S.W., *Surviving an Eating Disorder: Strategies for Family and Friends* (New York: HarperPerennial, 1997 (1988)), pp. 91–126.

14. *Diagnostic and Statistical Manual of Mental Disorders*, Fourth Edition (Washington, D.C.: American Psychiatric Association, 2000), pp. 583–584.

15. Ibid., pp. 589–591.

16. Ibid., pp. 785–786.

17. Ibid., pp. 507–509.

18. Pope, et. al. p. 120.

19. Ibid.

20. Dorie Krepton, "Weight Control," *Personal Trainer Manual: The Resource for Fitness Instructors* (San Diego, Calif.: American Council on Exercise, 1991), pp. 308–309.

Chapter 5. Treatments and Prevention

1. Harrison G. Pope, Jr., MD, Katherine A. Phillips, MD, and Roberto Olivardia, Ph.D., *The Adonis Complex: The Secret Crisis of Male Body Obsession* (New York: The Free Press, 2000), p. 145.

2. Ibid., p. 96.

3. Michele Siegel, Ph.D., Judith Brisman, Ph.D., and Margot Weinshel, M.S.W., *Surviving an Eating Disorder: Strategies for Family and Friends* (New York: HarperPerennial, 1997 (1988)), pp. 3–37.

4. Pope, Phillips, Olivardia, p. 170.

5. Drug InfoNet Doctors' Answers to "Frequently Asked Question," Anafril © 1996-97 DRUG INFONET, Inc., n.d., <http://www.druginfonet.com/faq/faqanaf.htm> (October 21, 2001).

6. Pope, Phillips, Olivardia, p. 100.

7. Personal interview with Wendy Nelson, registered dietitian, March 27, 2001.

8. Ibid.

9. Ibid.

10. Marion P. Olmsted and Allen S. Kaplan, "Psychoeducation in the Treatment of Eating Disorders," Kelly D. Brownell, and Christopher G. Fairburn, *Eating Disorders and Obesity: A Comprehensive Handbook* (New York/London: The Guilford Press, 1995), p. 300.

11. Timothy B. Walsh, "Pharmacotherapy of Eating Disorders," Kelly D. Brownell, and Christopher G. Fairburn, *Eating Disorders and Obesity: A Comprehensive Handbook* (New York/London: The Guilford Press, 1995), p. 315.

12. Pope, et. al., p. 235.

13. Siegel, et. al., p. 145.

14. Personal interview with Rebecca (real name withheld for privacy), March 15, 2001.

15. Wilson, Josleen, *The American Society of Plastic and Reconstructive Surgeons' Guide to Cosmetic Surgery* (New York: Simon and Schuster, 1992), pp. 49–50.

16. Ibid., p. 45.

17. Adapted from *Eating Disorders Awareness and Prevention list,* "Ten Steps to a Positive Body Image," 1999, n.p.; "20 Ways to Love Your Body!!" compiled by Margo Maine, Ph.D., 1999, n.p.; and Brenda Lane Richardson, and Elane Lehr, *101 Ways to Help Your Daughter Love Her Body* (New York: HarperCollins, 2001), n.p.

18. Ibid.

19. Siegel, et. al., p. 5.

Glossary

aerobic exercise—Exercise done over a period of time (20 to 60 minutes) that requires oxygen, such as walking, running, swimming, or biking.

airbrushing—A painting technique that eliminates imperfections but only in certain contexts.

amenorrhea—Loss of menstrual period.

amino acids—The building blocks of proteins.

compulsive—Repeating a behavior over and over with little purpose.

diuretics—Substances that increase urine output.

esophagus—The passage for food between the mouth and stomach.

genetics—The study of heredity and inherited characteristics.

heredity—The passing on of physical or mental characteristics from parent to child.

lanugo—Body hair often resulting from severe weight loss.

laxatives—Substances that increase output of the bowels.

metabolism—Chemical processes that result in energy output and growth.

obsessive-compulsive disorder (OCD)—A disorder characterized by repetitive thoughts and behaviors.

perception—The way something is understood or observed.

protein—A group of compounds of amino acids.

puberty—The time during which a person reaches sexual maturity.

repetition—In exercise, one complete movement. For example, in a bicep curl, the motion of lifting the weight until the arm cannot bend further, then lowering the weight until the arm is straight, is one complete repetition.

"roid rage"—Aggressive or violent outbursts caused by taking steroids.

set—In exercise, a group of repetitions.

supplement—In nutrition, something added to improve or make up for what is missing in the diet.

Further Reading

Frissel, Susan and Paula Harney. *Eating Disorders & Weight Control.* Berkeley Heights, N.J.: Enslow Publishers, Inc., 1998.

Lukas Ph.D., Scott E. *Steroids.* Berkeley Heights, N.J.: Enslow Publishers, Inc., 2001.

Madaras, Lynda, et. al. *What's Happening to My Body? Book for Boys: A Growing Up Guide for Parents and Sons.* New York: Newmarket Press, 2000.

Madaras, Lynda et. al. *What's Happening to My Body? Book for Girls: A Growing Up Guide for Parents and Daughters.* New York: Newmarket Press, 2000.

Moe, Barbara. *Coping with Eating Disorders.* New York: The Rosen Publishing Group, Inc., 1999.

Sneddon, Pamela Shires. *Body Image: A Reality Check.* Berkeley Heights, N.J.: Enslow Publishers, Inc., 1999.

Walker, Pamela. *Everything You Need to Know about Body Dysmorphic Disorder: Dealing with a Negative Body Image.* New York: The Rosen Publishing Group, Inc., 1999.

Internet Addresses

American Council on Exercise
<http://www.acefitness.org>

American Psychological Association
<http://www.apa.org>

United States Food and Drug Administration's Information for Teens
<http://www.fda.gov/oc/opacom/kids/html/7teens.htm>

Index

puberty, 9

R
Rembrandt, 7

S
serotonin, 10
  serotonin-reuptake
    inhibitors, 47
steroids, 20–21
  treatment, 49–50

warning signs, 42
supplements, 33–34
surgery, 50–51

T
tattoos, 36–38
teasing, 15

W
weight loss scams, 28–29